THE ELKS NATIONAL MEMORIAL

THE ELKS NATIONAL MEMORIAL HEADQUARTERS, CHICAGO, ILLINOIS

The Elks

NATIONAL MEMORIAL

AUTHORIZED BY
THE GRAND LODGE OF THE BENEVOLENT AND PROTECTIVE
ORDER OF ELKS OF THE U.S.A.
AND PUBLISHED UNDER THE SUPERVISION OF THE
ELKS NATIONAL MEMORIAL HEADQUARTERS COMMISSION
CHICAGO
1931

DESIGNED AND PRINTED FOR THE GRAND LODGE OF THE
BENEVOLENT AND PROTECTIVE ORDER OF ELKS OF THE U.S.A.
BY WILLIAM E. RUDGE'S SONS, INC., NEW YORK

PRINTED IN THE UNITED STATES OF AMERICA

CHARITY

MURAL PANEL
BY
EDWIN H.
BLASHFIELD

CONTENTS

LIST OF ILLUSTRATIONS

IN FULL COLOR

IN GRAVURE

FOREWORD

Many visitors to the Elks National Memorial Headquarters Building express a desire for a collection of views of the building, its interior and its art features, briefly described, together with some authoritative statement as to the purposes of the Memorial and the patriotic services thus commemorated. To meet this constantly growing demand, the Grand Lodge, at Miami in 1928, *directed the preparation and publication of this volume. It is issued in the hope that it will serve to accentuate an appreciation of the Memorial itself, and appropriately to disseminate information relating to the patriotic achievements of the Order and of its members.*

RECLINING ELK, BY LAURA GARDIN FRASER

THE ORDER OF ELKS

THE Benevolent and Protective Order of Elks of the United States of America was born in the minds and hearts of a small group of devoted friends, whose only selfish desire was for fraternal companionship and whose real aspiration was for an enlarged usefulness to their fellow man. For some time they had been banded together in a local organization of a purely social character. They were men of unusual intelligence, widely traveled, of deep earnestness, and of broad vision. Association in their modest little society had given them a fine conception of the splendid possibilities presented to a new fraternity which would be national in jurisdiction, charitable and benevolent in purpose, and essentially American in membership. Thus actuated and impelled, on February 16, 1868, in New York City, they formally organized the Benevolent and Protective Order of Elks.

The first steps in its development were, necessarily, hesitant and experimental; but they were set upon the path of a noble dream. Each succeeding stride was made with more confident assurance; and, as the Order grew, it was more and more definitely and wisely moulded into a great instrumentality of humanitarian service.

"To inculcate the principles of CHARITY, JUSTICE, BROTHERLY LOVE, and FIDELITY; to promote the welfare and enhance the happiness of its members; to quicken the spirit of American patriotism; to cultivate good fellowship; . . ." —thus does the preamble of the present constitution declare the Order's lofty purposes. From its inception it has remained faithful to these high ideals. It has consistently grown in numbers and in power; and by its benevolent and patriotic achievements it has firmly established itself in public confidence and esteem.

Its primary object being the practice of charity in its broadest significance, not merely that of alms-giving, it early adopted the policy of permitting its subordinate lodges to select their own particular fields of endeavor, rather than that of requiring them to participate in national projects undertaken by the Order as a whole. The wisdom of this policy has been fully demonstrated, and it has been generally maintained. Indeed the rule has been relaxed in only five instances, in each of which the objective was peculiarly national in scope and universally appealing to the entire membership.

The first of these was the establishment at Bedford, Virginia, of the Elks National Home for aged and indigent members. The second was the creation of a war relief fund, and its administration during the World War directly under the supervision of the Grand Lodge. The third was the erection and maintenance of the Order's National Memorial, in Chicago; and, concurrently, the establishment of the Elks Magazine as the official journal of the Order. The most recent was the establishment of the Elks National Foundation, for the furtherance of charitable, educational and benevolent activities, primarily in supplement to and in aid of those already under the administration of its local units.

Non-sectarian, non-political, drawing its members from all sections, from all denominations and from all political parties, the Order was naturally a medium through which those of differing creeds and political affiliations and sectional viewpoints would reach a better understanding of each other.

Organized at a time when the aftermath of the civil war was still apparent in sectional bitterness and prejudice which retarded the healing of old wounds and delayed the restoration of real national accord, the Order of Elks may justly claim a foremost place among the agencies which aided in the final destruction of those barriers and speeded the happy consummation of a truly reunited people.

It was the first, and is yet the only, fraternal organization to require by positive mandate that each subordinate lodge shall annually observe Flag Day with appropriate ceremonies. These recurring celebrations, instructive as well as inspiring, constitute a patriotic service to our country whose value and importance cannot be overestimated.

The prescribed memorial services held by each lodge on the first Sunday in each December, in memory of its fraternal dead, are uplifting and heart-cleansing occasions, quickening the finer sentiments and emotions. They have come to be recognized as annual events of general community interest in hundreds of cities and towns all over our land.

The several State Elks Associations, comprising the subordinate lodges in the

FRATERNAL JUSTICE
LUNETTE IN WEST CORRIDOR BY EDWIN H. BLASHFIELD

respective States, have committed themselves to benevolent projects of major importance. The treatment and training of crippled children, the prevention and cure of tuberculosis, the education of worthy young men and women, the maintenance of hospitals, and the establishment and conduct of playgrounds, may be mentioned among the many activities engaging the attention of these bodies.

The growth of the Order has been so marked that it now numbers its members in hundreds of thousands. The aggregate of its charitable expenditures each year is measured in millions. Its proved value as an instrumentality of patriotic service has led the national government again and again to enlist its ever willing and efficient aid. Its fraternal temples, of architectural beauty and of sumptuous appointment, have been builded wherever the American flag flies in sovereignty. Upon the altar in each one of these temples that flag is reverently draped as its first significant decoration.

It is not surprising that the Order of Elks has attracted to its membership the highest and best of American citizenship, who cherish its fraternal associations, who feel keen pride in its record of achievement, and who experience a deep satisfaction in their contemplation of its continuing service to our country and to humanity.

BRONZE DOORS—MAIN ENTRANCE

THE ORDER AND THE WORLD WAR

FROM its organization the Order of Elks was designed to be distinctively American, with a membership restricted to citizens of the United States. One of its chief aims has been not only to keep ever alive in the hearts of its own members a realization of the obligations of that citizenship, but also to quicken the spirit of true patriotism among the whole people. As might have been expected, therefore, the entrance of our country into the World War was faced by its members with a courageous loyalty and devotion, and with an eager readiness for sacrificial service that led them to a prompt and generous response to every call to patriotic duty.

Anticipating the desire of the Grand Lodge to take appropriate action, commensurate with the power and dignity of the Order, in aid and support of the common cause, the Grand Exalted Ruler, on June 2, 1917, appointed a special committee to take counsel with the federal authorities and their accredited agencies, to ascertain the manner in which its resources might most effectively be employed. This committee presented a report to the Grand Lodge, in session at Boston, on July 11, 1917, recommending that a special war relief fund be provided to be applied to such specific purposes, and in such manner, as might from time to time be deemed wise. The recommendation was immediately adopted; and, by a spontaneously unanimous vote, attended by outbursts of patriotic enthusiasm, the Order appropriated one million dollars to this fund; and authorized the appointment of the Elks National War Relief Commission to have full power and control in its administration.

The members of the Commission, having found it to be the most pressing need, as well as the most humanly appealing, immediately addressed themselves to the task of aiding in the adequate care of the sick and wounded fighting men overseas. Their first activity in this field was to provide for the complete equipment of two Base Hospitals: No. 41, organized from the faculty and alumni of the University of Virginia; and No. 46, organized from the faculty and alumni of the University of Oregon.

But for this timely aid from the Elks, no government funds having been provided for equipping such volunteer units, neither of these splendid organizations, of unexcelled personnel, would have been available for active service. Thus promptly financed, however, they were the first base hospital units to reach the battle area in France, where they rendered notably distinguished service.

As the maimed and wounded of our forces were brought back home in ever increasing numbers, their treatment and rehabilitation overtaxed the existing available hospitals and created an exigent need for additional facilities.

The Commission, after securing the grateful approval of the government, purchased a commanding site on Parker Hill, in the city of Boston, and erected thereon a reconstruction hospital of seven hundred beds capacity. It was dedicated with appropriate ceremonies, and turned over to the government, on November 16, 1918, being the first of such hospitals to be established in the United States. It was operated to full capacity, serving thousands of our wounded, until the need for it had passed in 1921.

The Grand Lodge convened at Atlantic City in 1918, with no less enthusiasm than was displayed at the 1917 session, appropriated an additional one million dollars to its war relief fund. Thereupon the Order tendered to the government another reconstruction hospital to be located at New Orleans. This offer was accepted and plans for it were prepared and approved. Before actual construction was begun, however, certain existing buildings in that city were found available and were acquired by the government, and the Order was thus denied the opportunity to perform this particular service. Shortly thereafter the armistice was signed; with it the need for the additional appropriation passed, consequently no call was made upon the membership to provide it.

During the early Summer of 1918 an appeal was made for the erection and equipment, at Camp Sherman, Ohio, of a much needed building in which the families of the forty thousand soldiers stationed there might be cared for during their visits to that camp. A thorough investigation of the conditions led to the approval of this project; and in October, 1918, a commodious community house, complete-

VIEW TOWARD LINCOLN PARK AND LAKE MICHIGAN, SHOWING BRONZE FLAGSTAFF BASE

ly furnished and equipped, was placed in commission, to meet this special need.

So well did it serve its purpose that as early as December 5, 1918, Captain James C. Netts, the officer in charge, reported:

"The Elks Building has done its duty already. It was finished in the early stages of the epidemic at Camp Sherman, and its 72 rooms took care of about 1000 mothers, fathers and relatives of the boys who were sick in the hospital. . . . If another guest never walks in its doors, it has been well worth while."

This useful adjunct of that great military camp remained in commission so long as the need for it continued.

In the meantime the Salvation Army, which was performing a wonderful work among the soldiers in France, earning the highest encomiums from officers and men alike, had undertaken a nation-wide campaign for funds. The Elks have always befriended the Salvation Army; the subordinate lodges all over the country were fostering this campaign in every city and state; and the War Relief Commission deemed it appropriate to add substantial assistance from the funds under their control. This they did by a cash donation of sixty thousand dollars.

The Order of Elks was the first fraternal organization whose aid was sought by the government in the national movement for food conservation. At the request of the food administrator, delegated representatives of the Order attended a conference with him in Washington, on August 2, 1917, having first been graciously received in special audience by the President.

As a result of this conference, and in accordance with the commitment there made on behalf of the Order, its members all over the country responded with enthusiastic unanimity to the appeal for proper food conservation. Three hundred thousand individually signed pledge cards were secured, committing the signatories to aid in this essential cause.

Perhaps the most distinctive service of the Order in war relief was in connection with the vocational training of our disabled heroes, a field which it had entirely unto itself in accredited association with the Federal Board for Vocational Education.

In June, 1918, the Congress enacted a law which was intended to provide suitable vocational training for all disabled veterans of the war. Unfortunately the terms of the act were not sufficiently comprehensive to accomplish its full purpose. It developed that there were thousands of most deserving and appealing cases for which no provision had been made.

The Elks War Relief Commission felt that the fund under its control could not be better employed than in caring for these exceptional cases. The Federal Board for Vocational Education welcomed this proffered aid and gratefully cooperated to insure the effective administration of the funds allocated by the Commission for this particular service.

Not the least important feature of this relief work, made possible by the aid

FRATERNITY

MURAL PANEL
BY
EDWIN H.
BLASHFIELD

from the Elks, was the publicity campaign found to be necessary to bring the opportunity for vocational training to the knowledge of those entitled to receive it, and to locate many of the individual cases not covered by the federal law. In numberless instances temporary maintenance was required pending decisions of the government as to eligibility of the applicants; and in many others the entire expense of the training was paid out of the Order's provided funds.

Realizing that a proper spirit of independence should be encouraged, and that loans would be preferred to charitable gifts, the commission created a revolving fund from which such loans might be made to disabled veterans, the repayments of which would enable a larger number of individuals to be thus aided.

Thousands of disabled soldiers, sailors and marines received vocational training, fitting them for useful and independent lives, who, but for the Order of Elks, could not have secured that training. These loans were made without security, and it is a fine testimonial to our veterans that, of the nearly forty thousand loans made, approximating seven hundred thousand dollars, every dollar was repaid, except in a few cases where death, or other intervening cause, made it impossible.

So essential was this particular service of the Order and so conspicuously effective was the method of performing it, that a representative of the Elks War Relief Commission was requested to explain the details of its operation before the Committee on Education of the House of Representatives. When this was done, the Honorable Simeon D. Fess, Chairman of the Committee, said:

> "The government certainly appreciates the work that the Elks organization has done. . . . Your example of a revolving fund is a very good one for the government to follow. However, that has never before been presented to us; for that reason the Committee owes more than the usual gratitude to you for coming to us and giving us this clear statement of the work of the Benevolent and Protective Order of Elks, in cooperation with the government."

As a result, the government eventually did follow that example, and created a revolving loan fund of public money to continue that service in the manner which had been inaugurated by the Elks.

Thus far the story of the patriotic services of the Order of Elks during the World War relates only to those which were undertaken by it as a national organi-

FRATERNITY

BY ADOLPH A. WEINMAN

In facade of south wing

PATRIOTISM

BY ADOLPH A. WEINMAN

In facade of north wing

zation. But the story must also include a brief recitation of the activities of its fifteen hundred subordinate lodges. Each one of them, in its own jurisdiction and meeting its own peculiar opportunities, splendidly maintained the highest and noblest traditions of the Fraternity.

In more than seven hundred cities, their homes and club houses were turned over, in whole or in part, for use as headquarters and work rooms for local war relief activities, in all of which the Elks themselves played a leading part.

Millions of dollars of lodge funds were used in the purchase of liberty bonds.

Other such millions were donated to the war relief funds of unrelated organizations engaged in patriotic service; and indeed every movement designed to promote the common cause was accorded active support and material assistance by these subordinate units.

This was notably extensive and effective in the case of the Salvation Army. In its local campaigns for funds to prosecute its war service in its chosen field, the Elks loyally sustained and supported it everywhere. In many cities, and in some entire states, the whole administrative cost of these campaigns was financed by the local lodges of the Order. Miss Evangeline Booth, Commander of the Salvation Army in the United States, requested the privilege of a personal appearance before the Grand Lodge in session at Atlantic City, in 1919, for the purpose of expressing to the Order her acknowledgment of the generous aid to her own organization. That privilege was accorded and, in the course of her inspiring address, she said:

> "The Salvation Army can never forget, or get away from, its deep sense of indebtedness and gratitude to the grand body of men that is before me this morning. . . . I say without hesitancy that our organization could not have achieved its exceptional success in this war but for the splendid, practical, tangible aid that was rendered to us by the Elks."

Thus vicariously the Order performed patriotic services comparable in magnitude and importance with those directly undertaken through its own instrumentalities.

In no instance did the Order, or any of the subordinate lodges, appeal to the public for funds to finance their respective activities, but every dollar thus employed was provided by Elks.

Because of the source from which it comes, and the occasion upon which it

THE EXTERIOR COLONNADE

was paid, one tribute to the Order may be selected for appropriate insertion here from the many which are treasured and carefully preserved.

Upon his triumphant return to America from the battlefields of France, General John J. Pershing, who has long been an Elk and has given many evidences of his interest in, and loyalty to, the Order, was tendered a formal public reception in the city of New York, on September 9, 1919. On that eventful occasion he withdrew for a time from his public appearance, in order to greet officials and members of the Order in the lodge room of New York Lodge No. 1. In his address there delivered, he graciously referred to his own membership in the Order, and said:

> "No one knows better than an Elk what the Order stands for; and realizing, as I do, just what the vows of an Elk require him to do, prescribing in many ways the conduct of his life, I can readily appreciate, and do appreciate, the great work that has been accomplished by this Order.
>
> "We who were fortunate enough to be sent to the battlefields of Europe to represent our people, felt that we had a united nation behind us; and I know of no organization or body of men whose patriotism, whose loyalty, and whose benevolence, have contributed in a greater degree to making that a possibility. We have felt not only the spirit of your patriotism, but we have felt the national benefit of your efforts to carry forward the principles for which America has stood in this war.
>
> "I am proud to be able to say this to you so soon after my return to the homeland; and I wish to congratulate you, and Elks everywhere, for what you have done."

The expressions from other authoritative sources, in praise and appreciation of the Order and of its outstanding service during the World War, have brought a thrill of justifiable pride to its entire membership, each one of whom had a share in that acclaimed record of achievement. Those expressions have come from the highest officials of the government and from executive heads of other benevolent organizations. They have been uttered in the halls of Congress; they have been embodied in official reports; they have been set forth in formal resolutions; they have been contained in commendatory letters; they have been the special subjects of public addresses. Together they constitute many golden pages in the history of the Order.

"Blessed Are They That Hunger and Thirst After Righteousness"

Mural Panel in Memorial Hall by Eugene Savage

A TORCHÈRE IN THE RECEPTION ROOM

BRONZE URN—EAST CORRIDOR

THE INCEPTION OF THE MEMORIAL HEADQUARTERS BUILDING

MORE than seventy thousand members of the Order of Elks had been in the service of our country during the World War. They had served in every branch of the military and naval establishments and in every rank. Over one thousand of them had made the last supreme sacrifice in that service and had laid down their lives in exemplification of that fidelity to the obligation of loyal patriotism and devotion to country which they had assumed at their fraternal altars. It was recognized as a clear duty, in accord with its every tenet, that the Order should provide a suitable memorial to those heroes whose valor and sacrifice had shed over it such a radiance of glory.

The character and form of that memorial had not been determined, but throughout the membership there was a definite desire that it should be a notable one, in every way worthy of the Order and of those to whose patriotic service it would stand as an eternal tribute. At the Grand Lodge session, convened at Chicago in 1920, opportunity was presented to go forward with the project in a manner that gave promise of a distinctive and unique result.

The Grand Lodge had directed the investigation by a special committee of the advisability of the establishment of permanent national headquarters, for the adequate accommodation of the Order's officials, in which its increasingly valuable records could be properly preserved and protected, and from which its business affairs could be more effectively administered. The resolution of reference was purposely made sufficiently broad to permit the study of this subject in connection with

"Blessed Are The Peacemakers"

MURAL PANEL IN MEMORIAL HALL BY EUGENE SAVAGE

that of the Order's great memorial, with the thought that the two objectives might be accomplished in appropriate combination.

The Elks War Relief Commission, to whom the whole matter was thus referred, after an exhaustive consideration of the many questions involved, were of opinion that the real purposes and desires of the Order's membership would be most satisfactorily attained by the construction of a great memorial building, itself a stately monument, which should contain distinctive features in fitting commemoration of the service and sacrifice designed to be honored, and in which, appropriately subordinated, the utilitarian features might be effectively absorbed. Accordingly, in their comprehensive report to the Grand Lodge, convened at Los Angeles in 1921, they suggested that general plan; and they specifically recommended:

> "That the suggested building be made definitely monumental and memorial in character; that the architectural design be so stately and beautiful, the material of its construction so enduring, its site and setting so appropriate and commanding, and its distinctive memorial features so artistic and dignified, that the attention of all beholders will be arrested, that the heart of every Elk who contemplates it will be thrilled with pride, and that it will for generations to come prove an inspiration to that loyalty and patriotism which the Order so earnestly teaches and has so worthily exemplified."

The report was received with enthusiastic acclaim; its recommendation was adopted and provided for by appropriate legislation, including an ample provision for estimated cost; and the Order was embarked upon the most ambitious and important enterprise of its history.

MEMORIAL HALL FROM EAST CORRIDOR

SELECTION OF LOCATION AND SITE

THE decision to recommend the establishment by the Order of a national memorial building with appropriate utilitarian features was reached in the confident assurance that it would meet the ready approval of the entire membership. The question of its location, however, was one upon which there was, in the beginning, a great diversity of opinion.

A number of cities eagerly sought the honor and distinction of being selected as the place in which the proposed memorial should be erected. Apart from the local pride which prompted them to submit and urge their respective claims, there were in each case certain distinctive advantages worthy of careful consideration, which were accorded upon visits of personal inspection.

The Commission were of the opinion, however, that no single aspect of the proposed undertaking was sufficiently dominating of itself to control the selection of a location; but that the choice should be determined in favor of that city in which the building would most completely fulfill all its designed purposes.

In view of the magnitude and character of the contemplated memorial, as a concrete expression of all that is highest and best in the Order, it was obvious that it should be located in a city of such size and importance that the largest number of people, and especially the largest number of Elks, would have opportunity to view it.

It was likewise apparent that the site selected in any location should be one which, for years to come, would be reasonably expected to preserve its relative importance and desirability as a setting for such a memorial; not one likely to be affected by probable shifting of local centers of commercial and industrial activities.

It was important that such a building should not be located where it would, for any reason, lose distinctiveness as an outstanding fraternal and patriotic monument.

There were also considerations of commercial and administrative importance to be taken into account. It was requisite that the location should be one from which the business affairs of the Order could be conducted with convenience and dispatch; and with proper regard to the number and relative locations of the subordinate lodges and members to be served.

Other questions of moment related to transportation and postal facilities, taxation, expense of construction and maintenance, cost of site, street frontages, relationship to other structures of similar character, and kindred subjects.

After a careful study of all these problems, the Commission were unanimously of the opinion that the proposed building should be located in the city of Chicago. They so recommended, and the Grand Lodge promptly confirmed this choice.

At the same time the National Memorial Headquarters Commission was created and charged with the duty and authority to select and acquire a suitable site in Chicago; to secure and approve plans for, and cause to be erected on said site, the projected memorial building; and to have full control and supervision of its construction, furnishing and equipment, and of its maintenance until final completion.

That Commission immediately addressed themselves to the selection and purchase of an appropriate site, and were fortunate in being able to acquire the particular lot upon which their unanimous choice had fallen. The property is situated at the corner of Lake View Avenue and Diversey Parkway, having a frontage of 393 feet on the former and 250 feet on the latter.

Facing Lincoln Park, immediately beyond which lies Lake Michigan, the chosen site afforded a spacious setting for the memorial structure to be erected thereon. From the converging boulevards the views of it would be most impressive; and the outlook from it, across the park and over the waters of the beautiful lake, would be charmingly commanding. In every aspect the site approached the ideal.

ENTRANCE TO NORTH CORRIDOR

VIEW OF MEMORIAL HALL FROM NORTH CORRIDOR

THE BUILDING

WITH an appropriate site acquired and an ample building fund available, provided by all members of the Order in equal participation, and recognizing that the entire membership desired it, the commission undertook to secure plans for, and the construction of, the most beautiful and imposing edifice that art could design and skill produce. They dreamed of one that would be accorded a place among the famed memorials of the world dedicated as tributes to everlasting ideals.

That they might be wisely guided in dealing with the many technical problems to be solved, the commission retained as their professional advisor, Colonel J. Hollis Wells, of New York, a distinguished architect of wide practical experience in building operations. His advice and counsel were of inestimable value from the initial stages of the undertaking until his death on September 24, 1926.

Prompted by the desire to induce the employment upon the task of the best thought and artistic skill of America's foremost architects, the commission invited a carefully selected number of them to participate in a competition to be held under the rules of the American Institute of Architects. In this competition each participant was required to submit a design and drawings for the proposed building, showing its general appearance and floor plan, and embodying the contemplated memorial feature in combination with administrative offices.

Seven of the most distinguished architects in the United States competed. Each one presented a design of such excellence that it might well have been adopted. But after a careful consideration of their respective merits, that submitted by Egerton Swartwout, of New York, was unanimously selected as the most beautifully distinctive and as most completely fulfilling the purposes to be served.

The completed building, in its general aspect, is unique. The central, dominating unit of the structure is circular, massive in proportions and surmounted by a flattened dome, 115 feet above the main level. Entered by a single great arched doorway, entirely encircled at a height of 38 feet by a stately colonnade, just below which is a belting frieze carved in high relief, this central building constitutes the distinctively memorial feature of the edifice.

On the north and south of this circular unit, and connected with it by gracefully columned enclosed passageways, are wings of identical, classically simple design, containing two stories of offices for administrative use. In the front end of each wing, otherwise unbroken by any opening, is a capacious niche in which is effectively placed a statuary group of heroic proportions.

The whole structure, raised on two broad terraces, with flights of steps, the main floor being ten feet above the street level, presents a commanding appearance from any approach. The combination of the massive circular memorial, with the lower rectangular wings of classic design, is distinctively novel. Nothing just like it has ever been built.

The architect, in describing the general design, said:

> "I might say it was classic, and more Roman than Greek; I would prefer to say it was modern, and that it was American. It is certainly modern in conception, and while it is classic, it is not archaeological. It follows along the lines of that adaptation of the classic which got such a noble start in this country just after the Revolution; the style used in the Capitol and other buildings in Washington. It is our national heritage."

The floor plan effectively maintains the general purposes of combining the memorial and utilitarian features of the building. The whole design is E-shaped, with the circular building as the middle prong.

The doorway constituting the only front entrance leads through a vestibule directly into the great memorial rotunda, a true circle, seventy-five feet in diameter. This, with the several short arcades leading to other parts of the building, occupies the whole of the massive central unit.

Directly in the rear, and entered through one of the arcades, is the reception room, seventy-five feet long by thirty feet wide. This is flanked on each end by a circular conference room, into which entrance is made through a doorway from the larger room. These three constitute what might be termed a rear wing, connected

"Blessed Are The Pure In Heart"

MURAL PANEL IN MEMORIAL HALL BY EUGENE SAVAGE

directly with those on the north and south, and forming the back of the letter E.

Wide passageways lead from the rotunda to the office wings, which are also accessible through the conference rooms. The north wing is conveniently arranged to accommodate the Grand Secretary and his clerical force, and to house safely the valuable records of the Order. Public entrance to this wing is directly from Diversey Parkway on the north.

The south wing provides commodious quarters for the Grand Exalted Ruler and other executive officers of the Grand Lodge, and for members of the staff of *The Elks Magazine*. Public entrance to this wing is from a private way leading in at right angles from Lake View Avenue.

Below the rotunda floor, and reached by broad curving stairways, are the spacious lounge, writing rooms, and other like facilities.

Across a wide alleyway at the rear, and abutting on Diversey Parkway, is the power and heating plant, which serves all the needs of the main structure.

The most cursory study of the general plan of the great edifice convinces one that it is the work of a master of monumental architecture. The numberless ornamental features show him to be a true artist.

Mr. Egerton Swartwout, the architect, for years had specialized in this type of architecture and had produced many examples of outstanding importance. But the Elks National Memorial Headquarters is his acknowledged masterpiece, to which has been accorded unstinted praise by his professional confrères and the general public alike as one of the great memorial buildings of the world.

THE CONSTRUCTION OF THE MEMORIAL

For so elaborate a structural undertaking, involving the selection of an infinite variety of materials and the consideration of a multitude of details, particularly relating to interior spacing and decoration and admitting of different treatments, the final working plans and specifications required long months in preparation and numerous conferences between the architect and the Commission. Upon completion they disclosed the need for such quantities of particular materials as to tax the capacities of the known sources of supply.

They called for a large tonnage of Indiana limestone, for the facing of the whole edifice, which must be satisfactorily uniform in tint and cut in thousands of

NORTH SECTION OF MEMORIAL HALL SHOWING SYMBOLIC STATUES OF FIDELITY AND JUSTICE, BY JAMES EARLE FRASER

SOUTH SECTION OF MEMORIAL HALL SHOWING SYMBOLIC STATUES
OF CHARITY AND BROTHERLY LOVE, BY JAMES EARLE FRASER

blocks of exacting shape and dimensions. They required such a quantity of Eastman cream-colored marble for interior facings that the possibility of securing it was seriously questioned. It was finally procured after the removal of two entire floors of the only quarry in which it is to be found. They called for other marbles, for monolithic columns and ornamentation, of such variety of color and texture that the quarries of the world had to be searched for them. Although the needs for other materials were less difficult to be met, the quantities involved and the rigid specifications as to quality, design and workmanship, presented real problems.

It was apparent that such a task should be entrusted only to builders of the highest repute, of proved ability, of wide experience upon works of real magnitude, and with an established organization equipped to handle the unusual requirements of this particular undertaking. The Commission were fortunate in finding all these qualifications possessed by Hegeman-Harris Company, Incorporated, of New York, to which the general contract was awarded in 1923.

The builders entered upon the task with an enthusiasm for the opportunity afforded and with a high purpose to meet generously every demand upon them. Colonel John C. Hegeman, president of the company, undertook personally to superintend the work; and under his aggressively efficient, but diplomatic, management all difficulties were successfully overcome. Predicted labor troubles failed to develop; exacting municipal regulations were administered without friction or embarrassment; factories and quarries, supply men and transportation agencies, all responded under his supervision to maintain a steady flow of required materials. Under his guiding hand the great structure grew apace into the thing of beauty that was the architect's dream.

The cornerstone was laid June 7, 1924, with impressive ceremonies conducted by the Grand Lodge officers, in accordance with the Order's prescribed ritual.

On July 14, 1926, as the principal event of the Annual Convention of the Order, held that year in Chicago, the building was dedicated by the Grand Lodge officers, in the presence of a vast throng of the members of the Fraternity. A special ritual was prepared for this unique occasion, one never before used and probably never to be observed again.

The structure thus put into commission is one of the most flawless combinations of perfect materials and master craftsmanship ever erected anywhere. From the huge blocks of stone to the smallest hidden details, everything is of the very best.

THE FEAST ON MOUNT OLYMPUS

CENTER PANEL IN TRIPTYCH IN CEILING OF RECEPTION ROOM
BY EUGENE SAVAGE

EXTERIOR ART FEATURES

THE memorial building, in its attractive setting, presents a picture that is of itself architecturally beautiful as well as imposing; and the surroundings, as well as the exterior of the structure proper, have been embellished by majestic sculptures and ornamental details which materially enhance its artistic value and importance.

Approach to the main entrance is made between massive stone pedestals, each of which supports a life-sized reclining elk, in bronze. Facing each other in duplicate postures of dignified repose, these representations of the gentle and graceful animal from which the Order derives its name, are strikingly faithful to the living models used, and symbolically indicate the fraternal significance of the shrine here established. This appropriate introduction to the memorial is the work of Laura Gardin Fraser, widely acclaimed as America's foremost artist in animal sculpture, and it was awarded first prize at the 1928 Exhibition of the National Arts Club in New York, as the best work of art by a woman, in either painting or sculpture, produced in 1927.

VOTIVE URN—CROWNING ADMINISTRATIVE WING

At the corners of the low coping wall which encloses the site, and at the north and south entrances, are duplicated massive stone urns carved in low relief which are a dignified contribution to the general ornamentation.

The terraced flights of steps are flanked by grassy parkings in the centers of which rise graceful flagstaffs, springing from elaborate bronze bases of artistic beauty. From these twin staffs there floats every day the American flag, emblematic of the loyal patriotism of the Order's membership.

Each of the administrative wings is capped, for a portion of its depth, by a low pyramid, built up of large blocks of stone, which is surmounted by a large votive basin upheld by conventionalized rams, also in stone. These form striking details of the architectural design, and, by their elevated, altar-like appearance, they convert these utilitarian units into appropriate components of the general monumental aspect of the whole structure.

DETAILS OF EXTERIOR LANTERNS

High above the main level, upon the face of the circular building, and to be seen between the columns of the great colonnade, are repeated stone panels, carrying distinctive designs carved in low relief. These are from the hand of the distinguished sculptor, Gerome Brush.

Peculiarly effective in their formal settings within the niches prepared for

LOOKING INTO WEST CORRIDOR FROM MEMORIAL HALL

them in the facades of the administrative pavilions, are the heroic bronze groups of Adolph A. Weinman. Without a superior among the world's living sculptors, Mr. Weinman is seen at his best in these groups, which are entitled, respectively—"Patriotism" and "Fraternity."

Patriotism is here represented in a composition of four figures of which Columbia, holding aloft the torch of liberty, her left hand extended in blessing, is the dominating motive. At her right are grouped a mother and boy, the mother relating the glorious history of their country, thus inspiring him with love and devotion to his native land. At the left of Columbia is a standing figure in the fullness of manly vigor, partly draped in the folds of the stars and stripes, and offering his sword and shield for the defense of his country. As a crowning feature of this group is an American eagle with outstretched wings, standing upon a branch of a spreading oak—symbol of power.

Fraternity, the companion group, also contains four figures, of which that representing Nature is the dominating motive. Kneeling at the left is the figure of an old man, looking up beseechingly to the sturdy masculine figure standing at the right and in benevolent gesture offering support to his brother in need. Behind the kneeling figure appears a youth, looking questingly into the partly veiled countenance of Mother Nature, whose extended arm rests gently upon his shoulder.

The background of this group is formed by columnar arbor vitae, above which appears as a crowning motive, drifting clouds and shining stars, the latter reminiscent of the old Arabic proverb: "The love of brother for brother is eternal like the stars." The spirit of the whole is that of benevolence and brotherly love, the encircling movement of the arms of all four figures recalling the touch of nature that "makes the whole world kin."

Appropriately and beautifully symbolizing the virtues which inspired the whole memorial, and to which it is a tribute, these great companion bronze groups are unexcelled in contemporary sculpture.

Approaching the massive central doorway, one sees, stretching to the right and left from its arched top, a majestic frieze. Five feet broad and one hundred and sixty-eight feet in length, it constitutes the most extensive work of its kind in the world, and is the distinctive art feature of the exterior of the monumental central unit. The subject of the frieze is expressed in the legend carved above the great door: "The Triumphs of Peace Endure—The Triumphs of War Perish."

PATHS OF PEACE

MURAL PAINTING
IN RECEPTION ROOM
BY
EUGENE SAVAGE

Beginning at the far right, the continuous procession of life-sized figures, carved in high relief, depicts the incidents of warfare which progressively and inevitably culminate in the allegorical figure at the front of this section, bespeaking war's futility. In contrast, the left section embodies a procession of men, women and children, engaged in the pursuits of peace, leading to the final figurative representation of resultant happiness and contentment.

This magnificent example of the sculptor's art is also by Mr. Weinman. In its conception and in the execution of its scores of figures, each one distinctively vital and individual, he has displayed true genius and has wrought another masterpiece to enrich his fame.

THE MEMORIAL ROTUNDA

THE arched doorway, affording the only access to the building from the front, is completely filled by great bronze doors. The design is elaborately ornate, cast in duplicate with heavy plate glass between, thus presenting the same finished appearance of open work from within and without; and yet the essential effect is that of massive strength. These doors, in striking contrast to the severely plain stone facing into which they are set, constitute one of the outstanding art features of the memorial. They are the product of the Gorham Studios and have been accorded recognition as among the finest examples of portal architecture.

Just within the doorway, one on either side, and set within deep alcoves faced with marble, are two unique works of art which are also highly utilitarian. Apparently heavy urns of bronze, carrying as their distinctive ornamentation a moving herd of elk in low relief, and resting upon heavily moulded bronze pedestals, they are in reality beautiful screens for the essential heating radiators within. They are also the product of the Gorham Studios and are novel in the adaptation of the highest art to such useful purposes.

Passing through a short, high ceiled arcade, one enters the great memorial rotunda. The first impression is that of sweeping spaciousness. The eyes instinctively turn upward to the vaulting dome a hundred feet above. There they rest for a moment upon the aluminum and gold central core, in an unconscious effort to solve the secret of the soft and golden, but effective, light that is diffused by it downward and outward from an undisclosed source.

Then the gorgeously colored, deeply set medallions, filling the remainder of

THE WEST CORRIDOR LEADING TO RECEPTION ROOM

the ceiling in concentric circles, force a consciousness of the wonderful richness, yet perfect harmony, of color everywhere. It is only after this experience of the general effect that one is able to seek out the details that contribute to it.

In every direction there is marble. The interior facing of the main walls and corridors, the great floor, the 24 huge columns forming an interior colonnade 27 feet above the floor, the 44 columns marking the corners of the arcades leading to other sections of the building, those which flank the niches containing the symbolic statues, the graceful balustrades protecting the stairways to the rooms below, the stairways themselves, the contrasting entablature and moulding around the walls, all are of marble. Nowhere in the world has there ever been such a quantity and variety of beautiful marble employed in any one structure.

Varying from darkest green and richest chocolate brown to the most delicately tinted light blues, lavenders and greens, exquisitely carved and perfectly polished, they are a feast to the eye to which the quarries of America, France, Italy, Austria and Greece have contributed of their best.

The massive upper columns, 30 feet from base to the top of their gilded Corinthian capitals, are most striking in their variant yet harmonious darker coloring, which is effectively repeated in the great discs and plaques of the rotunda floor, cut from the same quarries.

Uniformly spaced about the circular hall are four elaborately designed niches, in each of which, elevated upon an altar-like pedestal, is a statue in gilded bronze. They symbolize respectively the four cardinal virtues of the Order: CHARITY, JUSTICE, BROTHERLY LOVE and FIDELITY. These significant figures, of heroic size, are the work of James Earle Fraser, one of America's foremost sculptors. Admirably conceived to express their meaning and executed with perfect skill, they would find a welcome place in any one of the world's great art galleries.

Between each pair of the upper columns is a tall window of art glass, designed and colored to harmonize with the whole, while furnishing a softly filtered light to the interior of the memorial hall.

Alternating with the windows are twelve large panels which contain a series of allegorical mural paintings from the hand of Eugene Savage, whose work in this field is unsurpassed by any living artist. The number and size of these paintings presented a gigantic task upon which Mr. Savage was absorbedly engaged for years.

Most appropriately in such a memorial, his selected theme is the celebration

GENERAL VIEW OF RECEPTION ROOM

ANOTHER VIEW OF RECEPTION ROOM

of the spirit of bravery and sacrifice of those who gave their utmost to their country in the world war. The several panels, each with its own rich imagery and wealth of color so characteristic of this distinguished artist, depict the sacrifice and rewards attending that patriotic service, and the spiritual experiences of those who served, and those near to them who shared that great adventure.

Eight of the panels are based upon certain promised rewards in the Beatitudes. The remaining four are devoted to winged symbol-bearers carrying from the altars below the insignia of that virtue exercised in the different stages of the conflict.

Mr. Arthur Correy, President of the National Society of Mural Painters, has referred to these panels as: "The most important event in American mural painting." Altogether this masterpiece for which Mr. Savage was awarded the Gold Medal of Honor by the Architectural League of New York, in 1929, must be classed among the world's finest examples of mural art.

Below the interior colonnade, in the spandrels between the arched openings in the main wall, Mr. Savage has provided colorful subjects, significantly related to the great panels above. Fraternal altars, classically conventional figures, symbols of the chief branches of military and naval service, create an atmosphere that sustains and enhances the effect of the whole allegorical theme.

North and south, leading from the main hall into the passageways to the administrative pavilions, are short corridors, marked at each corner by twin columns of exquisitely tinted marbles, and having gracefully arched portals and ceilings in harmony with the general design of the rotunda. These effectively frame vistas of rare architectural charm and beauty.

Like corridors give approach to the stairways on either side, leading to the lounging rooms below; while suitably spaced alcoves of similar design provide a proper architectural balance to the whole.

Within the west corridor, leading to the reception room, are to be seen three beautiful paintings by the acknowledged dean of American mural artists, Edwin H. Blashfield.

To the right is a large panel filling the whole wall space, in which, with a perfection of drawing and charm of pose so characteristic of his work, the artist has presented a beautiful conception of Charity.

A flying figure with the horn of abundance is attended by others bearing gifts for the needy. In the lower center are supplicants, while a woman, represent-

ARMISTICE

MURAL PANEL IN
RECEPTION ROOM
BY
EUGENE SAVAGE

ing the spirit of the Order, in a gracious pose, seems to say to the flying figures: "Here are those who need. I commend them to you."

On the opposite wall, in a similar panel, is a group of men, in classic garb, each with uplifted arm above the central altar, assuming a fraternal obligation. Above in the bright glow of the altar fire stands a beautiful female figure holding aloft an olive branch symbolic of harmony. On either side of her sit figures holding fasces, typical of strength in union. In the lower foreground are two children with musical instruments, further suggestive of harmony. This panel is appropriately entitled Fraternity.

In the central lunette over the doorway is a beautiful group typifying Fraternal Justice. The figure of Justice is seated, not blindfolded, but with open eyes. About her three attendants bear symbols, a book, a sword, and balances. At the extreme left, gracefully posed adown the side of the door, is a figure bearing the mirror of introspection.

These three companion pictures are among the very best from the brush of this venerable artist. He has himself declared that he regards the lunette of Fraternal Justice as his finest production.

THE RECEPTION ROOM

THROUGH the west arcade, directly opposite the main entrance of the building, one passes into the great reception room. It is second only to the memorial hall in impressiveness; and, despite its size, it possesses a charming atmosphere of comfort, warmth and luxury.

The specially designed furniture, which contributes to that effect, includes two massive tables of walnut of exquisite grain and finish; ornately carved, high-backed chairs to match, and tall lighting standards in wood and bronze. Upon the floor, specially woven to fill their alloted spaces, are large oriental rugs in beautiful patterns and harmonious colors.

A distinctive touch of brilliance is added by four chandeliers of crystal and bronze, admirably proportioned to the spaciousness of the room and providing adequate night illumination.

Three large windows, deep-set in the west wall, of art glass specially designed and tinted to sustain the general effect, provide the soft daylighting of the whole

ART WINDOWS—WEST WALL OF RECEPTION ROOM

ENTRANCE DOORS OF RECEPTION ROOM SHOWING MURAL PANELS

interior. Contrasting with the dark woodwork all about, they are striking features of this unusual room.

The walls are high-panelled with dark English oak, against which are placed perfectly proportioned, fluted columns with Doric capitals of the same material. In the east face of this wall, on either side of the doorway, are two great panels, specially provided to contain companion murals.

Mr. Eugene Savage was commissioned to execute these and, choosing for his subjects "Armistice" and "Paths of Peace," he produced the masterpieces which occupy those panels and entrance every beholder by their appeal to the mind and heart as well as to the eye.

BRONZE GROUPS IN RECEPTION ROOM BY LAURA GARDIN FRASER

The former, on the right, contains a number of figures and is filled with action. The enormous canvas, in the richest of colors, depicts the delirium of joy attending the Armistice which brought cessation of strife in the World War. Soldiers are shown emerging from a trench, not yet realizing their release from its horrors. Others, striding along with laughing song, have lifted to their shoulders the framework of a belfry with its clanging bell, atop of which a French peasant girl is proudly seated, acclaiming her delight. In the center below, as a dominant figure, is an aged Madonna, with arms in the gesture of stopping contending forces, while she sorrowfully gazes upon the exquisitely painted figure of Truth, in the lower left fore-

NORTH CONFERENCE ROOM

ground, chained to a gun caisson. On the right, a shell-shattered shrine is shown falling from the chapel wall, the image of the patron saint partly fallen from its niche, yet still giving the traditional admonitions to a heedless world. Over the whole hovers a dove, emblematic of the peace to come, which is further indicated by a rainbow in the high background.

On the left, the artist has executed a no less colorful, but a more restful scene. In the background is a peaceful, far-stretching, agricultural landscape, with a beautiful blue sky above. In the foreground a completed family, from infancy to age, enjoy the bountifully harvested fruits of industry; while domestic animals, in contented well-being, share the general happiness of which they are an obvious part and to which they have contributed.

These companion pictures won also for Mr. Savage another Gold Medal of Honor awarded by the Architects League in 1930; and they are rightly regarded as special treasures among the many which enrich this patriotic and fraternal memorial.

Upon each of the large tables in the reception room is a small bronze group, from the hands of Laura Gardin Fraser, the sculptress of the reclining elks at the entrance of the memorial. Specially modeled and executed for their respective places, these companion bronzes are not merely table ornaments. They are superb creations of artistic genius.

One is a mythological, Minotaur-like beast, attended by satyrs. With arms folded upon his great hairy chest, and arrogantly pawing the earth with his cloven hoofs, he is the apotheosis of brute strength and physical passion.

The other, symbolizing the spiritual, is a gracefully soaring Pegasus, only clouds beneath his heels; while between his wide-stretched wings, with a single hand resting lightly about his neck, there is borne upward with him a beautiful youth, whose perfectly modeled body seems to require no support.

The most distinctive feature of the reception room is the wonderful ceiling. Gracefully arched, it is divided into deep panels of varying size and shape. Here again Mr. Eugene Savage, to whom was entrusted its artistic embellishment, has made the most of the rare opportunity afforded. With generous use of gold leaf and gorgeously rich colors, predominantly red, in fine harmony with the dark woodwork, he has created a canopy worthy of its setting.

In the smaller panels and spacings are repeated figures and decorative designs appropriately contributory to the main theme of the great mural in the center.

This is a triptych, filling the three large oval panels along the main axis of the ceiling. In resplendent colors, which the subject demands, it depicts a feast on Mount Olympus attended by all the gods, and derives its special significance from certain passages in the ceremonial ritual of the Order. For this reason it appeals with peculiar force to Elks, while its artistic excellence commands the admiration of all.

CONCLUSION

IT is difficult to avoid the constant repetition of superlatives in any properly appreciative description of the Elks National Memorial. The majesty of its architectural design, the beauty of its interior, its masterpieces of art, have led artists, poets, critics and laymen alike to acclaim its perfection and to accord it high place among the notable memorials of the world.

Truly a great dream has been realized in the beauty that has here been wrought. Truly a great purpose has been achieved in that all who behold it and realize its patriotic and fraternal significance, must be inspired to higher and nobler service to country and to humanity.

In no more beautifully chosen words could this be expressed than in the exquisite poem of O. L. Hall, Editor of the Chicago Daily Journal, with which he greeted the dedication of the Memorial on July 15, 1926:

THE ELKS MEMORIAL

There it stands—
Gazing out of golden eyes
At the emerald wood
And at the amethyst sweet water sea.
It is as the Roman Pantheon was
When the Pantheon was new;
Or it is Greece re-created,
In line as pure as ever was drawn
By Athenian architect to adorn
The high Acropolis.
Upon the very day of its creation

It presents to all the world a classic face;
To all the world it speaks:
"See, thou maker of ugliness,
How readily beauty comes from thy hands
When beauty is in thy dream."
This is a jewel of peace,
Bought with the blood of heroes;
The calm magnificence of its shining front
Betokens the fraternity
That has everlasting hatred of war.
So lovely a thing it is
That eye may not rest upon it
To be reminded of strife,
But only of beauty.